I Get
Knocked Down

A Woman's Survival Guide
to Business and Life

Eva Kalivas

Second Edition Copyright © 2008 by Evangelia Kalivas

NK Publications, Inc.
P. O. Box 1735
Radio City Station
New York, NY 10101-1735

www.nkpublications.com

ISBN 10: 0-9705100-4-7
ISBN 13: 978-0-9705100-4-4

Edited by Lisa Katcher

Cover illustration by Vicki Mamounas and Renee Mamounas

Printed in the United States of America

Contents

Dedication

Each of us receives various blessings during our lifetime. One of my blessings is the dynamic women that I have in my life. I dedicate this book to these women. Without you, I would not be who I am. My admiration, respect, love and genuine 'like' of these women has effected my life deeply and I thank them for that.

To my friends, Christine – for being my soulsister, for her caring and acceptance of people for who they are; Marie – for being the most grounded individual that I know; Maria – for her realness; Kathy – for her compassion; Antonella – for her kindness and a special thanks to Mamie, for her constant support and for the push that she gave me to finish this book.

To my cousins, Olga, Vicky, Irene and Jenny – for their individuality and strength; for being beautiful inside and out.

To my sister, Vicki, for being not only my editor and my illustrator, but for being the epiphany of a lady, keeping it real, not being afraid to laugh or to cry, and for most of all loving and caring about me as my 'big' sister. To my niece, Renee, for not only illustrating my book cover, but most of all, for her genuine encouragement after reading a draft of the book and immediately calling me to tell me how much she liked it.

And of course, to my mother. My mother is the strongest woman that I know. It's a strength that runs deep, both spiritually and emotionally. However, it is covered up with her simplicity, her appreciation of life, her love for her family and her acceptance of all people as a soul that should be respected and treated fairly in life.

All of these women are my rock, and I am forever grateful to have them in my life!

I have to thank my father as well. He is the man in my life that taught me that you can make an honest living by applying yourself and working hard at what you do. He taught me not to be greedy, to be ethical, to be responsible, to multi-task and most of all, to take pride in

what I do. I'm so proud of him and all he's
accomplished. ✺

Introduction

I've written this guide to share my career and life experiences that have often taken me on a rollercoaster ride. Let me summarize who I am today. In one sentence, I've been married, divorced, had to restart my career, have been laid off, started my own company, and live, on my own, in New York City. Life hasn't gone all that 'smoothly' for me. Some people can just coast through life while others constantly hit speed bumps. I'm just a speed bump magnet!

This book isn't a man-bashing guide. It's not a 'read this and get rich' guide. This book is intended to give you a little boost when you're feeling down about work. It's meant to motivate you as a woman; not just as a woman with a career, but a woman that is juggling twenty things at the same time.

By no means am I claiming to be an 'expert' in self-improvement. Far from it! One thing that I've learned in life is that we all have a story to tell. I'm simply sharing mine.

It took me almost six years to finish this guide. I've always enjoyed writing. Writing is one of my passions. However, this is the first time that I'm sharing anything that I have ever written. This guide really started out as more of a release of thoughts that I was putting down on paper for my own gratification and exploration. As I started to throw myself into my thoughts I realized I wanted to share my career experiences with other women. I have always enjoyed reading career motivational books and biographies. Such books have definitely inspired me throughout my career. I am a true believer that we can make the most of life's experiences by sharing them with others. You see, if you walk away with even one or two ideas, and one or two laughs, then this book has achieved its goal.

Now, let me start by telling you a little something about myself. I was born on the cusp of the two most opposite signs, Cancer and Leo. I grew up in a one-bedroom apartment in Astoria, Queens, with my older sister and my parents. For those of you familiar with New York City, Astoria is nicknamed "Little Athens".

I think there may be more Greeks in Astoria than there are in all of Greece.

We moved into a one family house when I was nine. I had my own room! My poor sister! She was six years older than me, and 15 when we moved out of the apartment into a house. She must have been dying to get her own room. I was oblivious. I remember sleeping on the floor next to her bed on many nights, especially the first year that we moved. What can I say? I missed staying up and talking all night (my nickname through elementary school was motor mouth).

It's a typical New York City story. I am a first generation American. My mother came here because her family lost everything to the Germans at the end of World War II. (Bet you didn't know that there were many territories in Greece that were devastated during the World World II invasions). She returned to Greece to get married, and returned to America with my father. My father came to America for the first time at the age of 26. Like every immigrant's story, they came here for a better life. So, he worked hard. He worked very hard. Like most Greek immigrants, he got involved in the restaurant business. It's a tough business. Lots of hours. I grew up in a very old-school environment. No summer camp, no sleepovers, no allowance...you get the picture. But there was definitely lots of love, simplicity and strong family values.

Where is this all heading? I've learned a lot with each rollercoaster ride. The old saying, it's not easy being a woman, is true. I think it's even harder being a woman raised with very traditional values working in a very modern and aggressive man's world. When I say 'harder', I mean perhaps more challenging. Who am I to say something is 'harder' or 'tougher'? We all have our own definitions in life. Working in a man's world is something that, for the most part, my generation has had to learn on our own. Most of our mothers were homemakers (a.k.a. housewives). Most working mothers worked fields predominately set aside for women; such as a teacher, as a nurse or as a secretary. It was a whole new world out there for our generation.

Of my 13-year 'full-time' career (I started as an intern in my sophomore year of college), I have always worked on commission and have never worked 9-5. There was actually a year I did work for a base salary plus commission. That felt foreign to me.

I'm a financial consultant. I started out as a cold caller at the age of 17. Being in 'sales' is hard enough. Selling a service or your expertise and not a product is exposing yourself to the mother load of all rejection! I mean it. Women, as a gender, have a hard enough time dealing with rejection. Can you imagine dealing with it everyday? How about dealing with it all day at the very start of your career? I always say ignorance is bliss. It is not a coincidence that most financial advisors that make it and stay in this business start out young in this field.

Please do not for a moment think that I cannot relate to any other careers besides my own. I've been on the sales end, I've been a manager, I've been my own administrative assistant for the majority of my career and I now own my own company with a business partner.

I'm not saying that I'm Superwoman! I'm far from it. As you read on, you will realize that I'm just one of those people in which 'nothing comes easy'. I have fallen, risen, changed, evolved, and taken chances. I've done this all out of both pure necessity and drive, combined together.

So, please sit back, get a cup of coffee or a glass of wine (I don't want to hear any preaching about caffeine and alcohol...some things are all about moderation), and enjoy. I hope that my life experiences help all of you cope, grow, and learn something that will help you in your career trials and tribulations.

Chapter 1

Some Things Can't Be Explained

Isn't it funny how siblings, raised by the same parents, in the same manner, can have such different personalities? One of the things that I've accepted, slowly over time, is that I haven't really changed all that much from the way I was as a child. Of course, I've matured, but my core personality traits are still intact.

I was always very independent and outgoing. I was always very sensitive and analytical. We go through our lives, trying to figure out why we are the way we are. Do not dwell on this. I feel that it is so much more productive to work with your inner personality strengths and recognize your inner personality weaknesses. Naturally, being honest with yourself is the most important step in this process.

As women, we tend to be very aware of our weaknesses and tend to be modest about our strengths.

*There is nothing wrong
with a little ego, ladies!*

Some of us have great people skills, others great organizational skills, and so on. Chances are these skills shined through as a child. Go with your inner self.

As I mentioned in my introduction, my father had his own restaurant by the time I was two years old. I started asking my father to take me to work with him from the age of four. I loved it! It got me out of the house (this was way before internet access and playstation). I talked to different people all day. I continued to work with my father during the summertime and weekends, up until my early twenties. My older sister, however, never showed any interest in working at the restaurant. Why is this? We were raised by the same parents, in the same fashion. Different things make us happy. We have different goals, even as children, teenagers and young adults. Don't lose that in yourself. Life often beats us up. Don't forget what it is that makes us really tick inside. ♓

YOU HAVE TO BELIEVE IN YOURSELF!

Chapter 2

Stay Grounded

One of the things that I have found to be very helpful is keeping in touch with my childhood friends. It really does help keep me grounded and sane. We often lose sight of what we wanted out of life. Our friends, and I mean our good, solid friends, help remind us of who we are and where we want to go. We all dreamt of how our lives would be. We've sat around and talked about these dreams with our childhood friends for hours and hours. Even though your lives may be very different today, keeping in touch helps you stop and remember those times and those dreams. A simple phone call or birthday card is all it sometimes takes to help transport you just for a few minutes.

It is so hard to stay grounded. So much is expected from us. Women today are expected to have careers, be a size 4, look 10 years younger, keep up with all of the trends, have relationships, have families, be responsible... we have to do it all, and often put pressure on ourselves to do it well. It is very easy to lose your mind and lose yourself.

I found that a solid circle of friends has helped me get through a lot of tough times. Show your vulnerabilities to those that love you. If you don't, you'll end up showing them to the wrong people at the wrong times. We've all cried in front of someone that we didn't want to cry in front of; our boss, our manager or a co-worker. Most of the time, it has happened because of something unrelated to that moment in time.

Staying grounded
helps me stay focused.

*Staying grounded
helps me achieve my goals.*

*Staying grounded helps me
get through everyday life.*

Share yourself with those that you can trust and that truly like you, for who you really are. I'll give you a quick story. I had gained weight at one point in my life. I gained 25 pounds. I never had a problem with my weight. I always ate healthfully, because I like to, and enjoyed working out. Well, I was going through a major crisis at the time. I mean, MAJOR. I had just gotten divorced a year earlier, was living on my own, for the first time and had resigned from a company that I was with for six years. So, what did I do? I ate and ate and ate.

I succumbed to eating food that I never even had an urge to try: cookies by the box; ice cream by the half-gallon; pizza; Chinese food; burgers.

I ate everything!

I ate alone, sitting in front of the TV, ashamed. For those of you who have never fallen victim to this, trust me, it is the worst feeling. You eat because you're ashamed. You keep eating because you're angry with yourself for being weak and eating in the first place. Anyway, (let me move on, this can be a whole other book), I finally hit bottom one night. It was about 11pm and I was home, in front of the TV. I wanted cookies. Of course, there was no food in the house because I had eaten it all. But there was a late night mini-market open two blocks away from me. I threw my sneakers on, a jacket over my pajamas, and ran out to the store. I returned with the cookies, but had left my house keys home! I had taken my car keys by mistake.

I was locked out.

I didn't know what to do.

So, I sat on my stoop and ate all of the cookies (why let them go to waste?), feeling sorry for myself. I finally realized that I had no choice but to drive to my sister's house, wake her, her husband, and children, and explained to her that I had gotten locked out. I didn't tell her the story behind it all. I didn't tell anyone for a few days.

I had hit bottom.

I had to get myself grounded again and move forward. Within one year I had gone through a divorce, moved back in with my parents for four months, moved out of my parents' house into my own apartment, lived by myself for the first time in my life, and, to top it off, I was no longer working at the only full-time job I knew. Here I was, jobless, with no motivation, and feeling very betrayed and disappointed by the finance industry. As much as I wanted to just stay in my apartment in my sweats all day, one thing was certain - I had to find a new job. I had to pay my bills.

I realized that I not only had to find a new job, but most importantly, I did not want to feel as if I failed in my career.

I wanted to move forward.

My friends all knew that I was struggling emotionally at that time. No one really knew how bad it had gotten.

So I told everyone about the cookie story. I finally talked about the fact that I was sulking at home for the last few months. When I say everyone, I mean that I told my close friends - friends that love me.

Reaching out and talking about my vulnerabilities and insecurities helped me regroup.

*Sharing my vulnerabilities
helped me get over them.*

I found humor and relief in being vulnerable and in not being perfect.

I had let the big secret out. It gave me my confidence back.

I got my resume together and started going on interviews.

We're not perfect. Our friends and family know that best. I revealed myself to them. They helped me cope. They made me laugh. They shared their personal and professional outlooks with me. They shared stories with me about their career mishaps. They reminded me of some great memories. They believed in me.

I moved on.

Find the humor in life. We all go through it. Let's talk about it. 👜

I HAD GOTTEN KNOCKED DOWN!

I HAD TO PICK MYSELF UP AND MOVE ON!

Chapter 3

The Master Plan

Writing this chapter probably required the most courage. It's about the 'Master Plan'. As an ambitious woman, this Plan is our dirty little secret. We're somewhat embarrassed by it. We don't talk about it with anyone.

What I'm referring to is our urge to be 'normal'. When I say 'normal', please don't misconstrue it. I mean our plan to have the knight in shining armor (sometimes this can even be a husband), the children and the family life. C'mon, admit it...how many of you chose your major in college because it would be a good career for you to be in if, and when, you have a family. For example, most teachers that I know chose to become teachers with the primary reason in mind that it will be easier for them when they are working and have children, even though most of them did not have children yet when beginning their educational studies. I am not by any means knocking any profession. I think that the majority of women consider these factors.

My parents were not pleased with my choice to major in business because it was not, and is still not, a 'working mother' friendly environment. They wanted me to be a pharmacist or physical therapist, or to major in some type of profession that offers part-time hours, if needed. But I pushed forward and majored in something that I had in interest in - Business Management. I was tough, and I stood my ground. So, what did I do when I graduated at 22? I took a full time job at an office that was about 2 miles away from where I grew up.

Aaaaaaaaaaaah!!!

I did this because I thought it would be easier for me to have a family and continue to work if I lived near my parents. As independent and rebellious as I thought I was, it was too late – I was already programmed.

I think most of us have at one time or another in our careers felt this pressure to work in the business world and somehow conquer this 'Master Plan'. When I decided to write this book, I consulted with a number of professional women about this concept. I wanted to make sure that I wasn't the only crazy one for feeling this way. I found out that I wasn't. Many of these women secretly felt the same way. They too had a 'Master Plan'. So what do we do?

Now, into my thirties, I've re-evaluated 'the Plan'. I realized that things did not go exactly the way 'the Plan' was suppose to go when I graduated from college. I'm in my early thirties, not yet married, and not yet a mom. So I decided to get riskier with my career choices. I would cross that 'family' bridge when I get to it.

My career decisions for the past few years have been based solely on my present situation.

They have not been based on a future that I obviously am not yet living.

I started making my best career decisions when I finally realized that it was OK to deviate from 'the Plan'. I still want to have a family of my own. There will be some new career decisions that I'll address at that time. But I do know that I love what I am doing presently.

*Now I set my future goals
around my present life.*

I cannot stress how important this is. It takes really getting to know yourself and being very honest with yourself to finally get over the anxiety of letting go of 'the Plan'. Before I let go of it, I was much more cautious about making changes in my career path. I had taken the safe route, but, with time, I realized that the 'safe route' should not mean not making changes and taking chances. There's a difference between the 'safe route' and the 'scared route'. It is really all about what makes us happy and helps us achieve the goals that we have for ourselves in our careers.

In my twenties, I created goals around the 'what ifs' of having a family. I soul searched and realized that this was stopping me from really pursuing a more courageous career path. I started setting more aggressive, yet achievable, goals. I started asking myself 'what do I want to do when I grow up?' and I started doing it.

I think that in order to achieve this balance within ourselves we have to first confront the truth behind our fears and insecurities, and talk about them with other professional women. I always felt like I had to hide this feeling way deep down so that the men that I worked with didn't smell the fear. I had to fit into the 'boys' club'. Wanting to be a mommy and a wife was a big no-no. I can't go back in time and implement this confidence now. All I can do is use it as I go forward.

This ties into not being afraid of change.

Not everything in life goes according to plan.

The old saying, 'roll with the punches' has a lot of significance. Focus on where you want to go long-term, but implement mini-plans on how to get there based on 'the now', not 'the tomorrow'. It's a lot simpler to change or edit these 'mini-plans'.

Things may happen along the way that forces us to make some changes. We may willingly want to make changes. Keep asking yourself, where do you want to be in a year? Three years? Five years? Write these goals down and look at them at least twice a year. Don't just ask yourself, where do you want to be in ten or twenty years? Setting such a long time frame may restrict you from growing and changing.

Change should be welcome!

*That's why short-term goals are
just as important as long-term ones.*

Speaking of change, there are so many events
that can take place in both life and at work
that we will never be able to plan for. Writing
about such life events would require an entirely
separate book.

I'll just stick to the work events.

Companies get acquired. New positions
are created. Current positions are eliminated.
Departments come and go, as do supervisors
and managers.

Such events can only be deemed as negative
events if you choose to explore them in a
negative manner.

Changes and events at work may seem negative at first, but it is the outcome that should most concern you.

I'll give you an example. I did end up getting a new job in the finance industry. I took several steps back, both in position and in salary, but I did what was necessary for me to get back into the industry. Within a year, I was offered a challenging position at a major financial institution to create and run a new division. I jumped at the chance to do so. Within three months I had a department hired. Within six months I was producing revenue for the company.

However, corporate politics and power struggles prevailed.

By the ninth month, my entire department, including myself, was terminated. Laid off is a much nicer term, but I didn't see it coming. At this point there was only one thing left for me to do.

Calling it quits and looking for a new career was not one of them!

I had faith in myself.

So I followed the American dream – I started my own company. My counterpart at my prior company had also been laid off. I approached him about taking 'our show on the road'. In other words, take control of our destiny and put our experience to use for ourselves.

Together, my counterpart and I had the experience in the industry. We had made some great contacts through the years. Maybe it was the entrepreneurial side of me that took over after watching my father at work for so many years. He was his own boss. He placed his ability to earn an income and support his family in his own hands.

Within three months of being laid off, we found a new office, brought over our best employees and basically put together a company. EPIC Consulting, LLC was born! We were fortunate to have a great staff of employees believe in us and in our company vision. Six months into starting our company we were turning a profit.

I realize that being laid-off could have been a negative event only if I had decided not to do anything about it. It was that push that I needed to finally take the initiative to start my own business.

I had always worked hard.

Why not work hard for myself?

I'm sharing this with you to point out what I mentioned earlier in this chapter.

Events cause change.

IT IS WHAT WE DO WITH
THIS CHANGE THAT MAKES
THE EVENT EITHER POSITIVE
OR NEGATIVE.

Chapter 4

Expect the Unexpected

A year has passed since writing the last chapter and beginning this one. Wow, has a lot changed since I worked on chapter 3. Last time I was writing this, I was getting ready for my summer vacation. I returned from a two-week trip in August 2001, feeling great.

Then the world changed...September 11, 2001.

I was born and raised in New York. I live and work in the city (my office is in the Empire State Building). Like everyone else in America, I felt like I was living a nightmare watching the towers collapse. But, living in NYC, it really hit home.

I lost a childhood friend on that day. She was the sweetest, gentlest human being.

That day forever changed so many people's lives. Born out of that day, were so many powerful emotions to be felt and dealt with.

Professionally, I never had thought I would have to struggle again, like I did earlier on in my career. I had 'paid my dues'. Those days were over. Was I in for a rude awakening!

At this point, my company was nearing its second anniversary. Our office lease would be expiring November 2001. I had to look for new office space.

I had to stay focused.

Our clients were obviously very concerned. The core of our business is based on consulting mid and large size companies on their corporate

Retirement Plan Programs. An example of such a Plan is a 401k Plan. The majority of our clientele is nationwide. They were concerned that our office, located in the Empire State Building, was now a prime target for terrorism. We had to make sure that they did not sense our concerns. We decided to stay in the Empire State Building, more out of pride than anything.

We even moved into a much bigger, much more expensive suite. Looking back, I now know that this was a mistake we had made as business owners. This mistake was primarily due to our inexperience, not in our lack of knowledge in our profession, but our inexperience in running a company.

EPIC Consulting was just turning two years old. A word of advice, never take on a larger expense after a major world tragedy! We continued to work and stay focused. As the months rolled on, we realized that our country was holding its breath for the next tragic event to take place in New York City. We were a terrorist target. There was no chance of us closing any new business until the New Year.

We just kept focused.

We rang in 2002, and hoped that we could put everything behind us. Unfortunately, the economy just kept tumbling, and so did our bank account. My partner and I worked harder this year than ever, and made less money to show for it.

We did not close a new piece of business for one year.

We had employees to pay.

We had to act upbeat and positive everyday when we walked into the office.

The bills started to pile up.

We had to do some creative accounting (not the Enron type).

We took out some loans. We started to depend on our credit cards for our livelihood. To put it simply, we were going under.

I finally cracked in August of 2002. I had to face the possibility of losing the company. I had to face the possibility of 'failure'. In my kitchen at home, I have a tiny plague hanging on my wall that says, 'In every trouble there's a blessing.' I believe that now more than ever. I would have had a breakdown, if I had not already been through so many professional trials and tribulations. At the time, I would keep asking myself, 'Why me? Why again?' However I think it helped me build the thick skin that I needed to get through that last year and a half.

My partner was living in denial. I had to finally address him and seriously talk about the possibility of going under. I had no money in my pocket to preoccupy me, I was up to my ears in credit card debt, and I had to, worst of all, face the possibility of having to work for someone else again.

For anyone that is self-employed, we all know that it's more about the failure aspect than it is about the employment status. I did what any entrepreneur would do – I cried my eyes out. But I also did the very mature thing and opened up to those people around me that I knew loved me.

I swallowed my pride. I told my family and a small number of close friends what was happening. I remember breaking down one night in front of a friend. For the most part, my friends had no idea what was happening in my life financially. My friend listened. My friend's words reminded me that I had a loving family and that I had a number of people in my life that loved me. I have to tell you, at this point I didn't want to get out of bed anymore. I didn't know how I would go on.

But I was doing this all in private. I would be a 'working woman' during the day, and miserable and alone at night.

I began isolating myself from everyone. Opening up was overcoming a large obstacle. It was a cry for help. I needed to be reminded that I had people in my life care about me. It gave me strength. It helped me ask for help. I wasn't going through it alone anymore.

My friends would wish me luck before my appointments. They would take me out to dinner. It reminded me how important it is to take the time to build ties in your life. That's all that counts in the end.

I asked my parents for help for the first time in my life. They helped me in any way that they could. They knew it was serious, because I had never asked them for money before in my life.

I had to realize that pride would only get in the way and destroy me at this point.

Admitting a struggle or a failure is the only way to survive it.

We had enough in company funds to keep us afloat until October 2002. My partner and I hadn't paid ourselves in months. But we made sure to always pay our bills and our employees.

One thing I cannot stress enough is good credit.

In this day and age, ruining your credit is suicide. Good credit is what kept us afloat.

The one-year anniversary of September 11 came. I mentioned that I lost a childhood friend in the tragedy. On the one-year anniversary of 9/11 I met with her mother. Everyone was still in mourning and still in shock. It all still seemed so surreal. But, I had a business flight to catch and had to stay focused. I felt like an actor. I would have to pump myself up before each appointment. I would have to go and look happy and positive, when inside, I was crumbling. People smell fear. I couldn't let my prospects know that I was desperate.

We closed our first case in over a year on September 12th 2002. After that, we closed four more cases in four weeks.

I think what was most important, is that we kept focused and kept working hard. We didn't change what we were doing in the past...we just had to do a lot more of it. I am a big believer in 'if it's not broken, don't fix it', especially in business. Trying to reinvent yourself is not a bad thing, but trying to do it during desperate times is a lethal combination.

We stuck to our roots. We prospected, we pitched and we finally sold. I turned to my roots during this time more than ever. I had to implement all that I had learned through out my life, personally and professionally, to get through each day.

I had to avoid denial.

All we can do with our life experiences is learn from them and share them. If we don't do this, then life is not being lived to the fullest.

Our company had survived!

Surprisingly enough, so did I!

Chapter 5

Keep Your Personal Problems / Issues Our of the Office

I'm sure you all heard this a number of times. And yet how many of us work with those individuals that just seem to be buried down with personal problems and crises that you know all too much about.

Ask any employer or manager and they will tell you that it only takes one negative apple in the bunch to turn an entire bushel sour. For some reason, negative energy at the workplace (and out of it as well) streams much more aggressively than positive energy does. A negative employee is a manager's worst nightmare.

I'm going to continue to be brutally honest in this chapter. Very often at work, those around you may simply be waiting for an excuse or a reason for you to fail. The last thing that you want to give them is ammunition.

There is no reason for your co-workers or manager to know every personal crisis that you are having.

What your manager cares about is getting the work done and meeting his/her objectives. Your manager, your supervisor, your employer have a job to get done. If you are that person, and are responsible for a team of employees, that's even more reason to keep your personal problems at home. It will become a roadblock in your career.

I'll give you an example. When I was going through my divorce, I was working at a company that I had been with for five years. I was a sales manager at the time. No one knew I was going through a divorce until it was final, and I had to notify our office manager to take my ex-husband off of my health insurance. That's all it took. The news spread like wild fire, but at that point it was done. My manager, my peers, my sales reps were never given the opportunity to 'use' my divorce as an excuse for a bad day at the office, a slow sales week, or whatever normally happened at work.

My point is, there are people who pounce at the chance to kick you when you're down. They use your personal problem as a reflection of your work, even if they are completely unrelated.

It just is not professional to drag it into the workplace.

Don't get me wrong, we have all had a bad personal day affect us at work. We're human! It's ok and tolerated and understood from time to time. That is very different from airing your dirty laundry constantly. After a while, no one wants to hear it. After a while, it begins to get used against you.

Getting divorced was not easy. What would have been even harder was getting divorced and being scrutinized at work at the same time. Separating the two helped me display a level of professionalism (and strength) to my manager and more importantly, it set an example for my sales staff to hopefully follow.

Talking about my insecurities outside of work helps me stay more focused while at work. Our personal insecurities and emotions should try to be dealt with outside of the workplace. We need to stay focused at work. I, for one, need to keep going, keep selling, and keep managing. I, along with everyone else, need to do this, even though we may be going through some rough times personally.

Staying grounded personally helps me stay grounded at work. I found that this is much more effective than trying to ground myself by drowning myself in work. It's the other way around. Staying grounded personally helps me stay motivated. It helps me stay creative.

It's ok to share your vulnerabilities. Take the time to hear yourself talk out loud. Just try and keep the sharing and talking outside of the workplace. It will result in less stress and better productivity at work.

Chapter 6

Time Management

What would a 'business/motivational' book be without a chapter on time management? Now, for those of you that are working and have children, and about to read this, maybe you should just skip to the next chapter.

Just kidding.

I am not even worthy of speaking of time management in comparison to a working parent, particularly a working mother. However, being single is tough, too, (stop laughing). In all seriousness, I'm going to focus on time management with respect to work and your own well being.

If there is one thing that I've always tried to instill in anyone that I've managed or trained, it's to be organized. Here are some pointers that have always worked for me:

* ❈ Always organize your desk at the end of the day before going home. It takes an extra few minutes, but will keep you much more productive the following day.

* ❈ *Do not procrastinate!* I cannot stress how important this is. Manage your time as if you were managing an entity. If a piece of paper comes across your desk, look at it. If it can be taken care of in a matter of seconds, or minutes, just do it. Take care of it right there on the spot. The only time I do not do this is when I'm in the middle of something that requires

my full concentration. Then I put it on the side, and take care of it when I'm done. I try and leave the office without a 'to do' pile for the next day. That's why taking care of something on the spot, if possible, is so imperative.

✳ *Manage your priorities*. Have some type of work routine in place. I am so tired of people complaining that they are so busy at work and that they cannot keep up with their workload, as they surf the Internet all day. Take care of your priorities first, whether business or personal. Many of us put priorities off because they are more time consuming or mentally challenging.

✳ *Tackle your projects in order of priority.* At the start of the day, you should mentally have a pretty good idea what your workday will consist of. 'Surprise projects' are thrown in, and should be worked into your day.

✳ Here's an example:

My first hour at the office is a routine for me each day. First, I check my voicemails and read my work-related e-mails. I respond to the important e-mails and important voicemails first.

Then I look at my day planner. I have each day planned. I have a pretty good idea of what the day will consist of because I organized myself the night before.

I start my workload.

In between, I answer the less important e-mails and voicemails, and I keep my personal e-mails very limited.

I look at my mail each day when it arrives. I throw junk-mail out, right on the spot.

I pay my bills and take care of all banking issues weekly, on the same day of the week.

I have a routine.

That's what I want you to get out of reading this. Each of our routines will differ, according to our jobs. But, regardless, *try and create a routine around your workday. This will make you much more productive.*

⁂ *Write things down.* Yes, technology is great, but sometimes, it's quicker and easier to write things down. As I mentioned in a prior bullet, make a list at the end of the day of what needs to get accomplished the following day.

✳ *Manage yourself.*

✳ *Manage your time.* In this day and age, we are all so busy trying to keep up with the rat race, that time management is imperative to our productiveness and our sanity.

✳ *Don't put yourself last!* I'm still working on this one. You know the saying, 'the shoemaker is the last one to fix his shoes'. Many of us put ourselves last mentally. You have to make 'me time'. Many of us think that 'me time' has to be an all day event. It doesn't. Most of us don't have a day to commit to just ourselves. So make it an hour. It's better than nothing.

✸ *Make your health a priority.* Take care of yourself. Go to the gym. I can't stress this enough, especially for people that work on commission, or have a very high stress job. Your brain works better when your body does. Don't workout for vanity purposes. Do it for your mental well being. I use to encourage my sales reps to go to the gym during 'downtime'. It will make you more productive in the end. It's better to workout for an hour during the day, than to surf the net for an hour.

Do not put your health last. Too many of us do this. We're too busy to get sick. We're too busy to go to the doctor. Well, we have to make time for ourselves. I got sick more in the last year in a half, than I have gotten sick in my entire working career. It is not a coincidence! I had one of my most stressful work years ever. I was flying a lot for business. I was trying to get over 9/11. I was worn down. I remember I was fighting a cold for about 2 weeks. Of course, I didn't have time to be sick. I squeezed in a doctor's appointment, was prescribed antibiotics and then, did what I'm sure many of us do...I didn't finish them. I was still feeling congested and sick, but decided, of course, to still go on my business trip. Rescheduling or cancelling was just unimaginable; not even a thought. I learned my lesson. As soon as we landed in Greenbay, WI, I was rushed straight to the emergency room. The moral of the story is: make your health a priority. Trying to be 'Superwoman' can be overrated.

* Don't spend a lot of time on things that are not very important or significant. How many of us have witnessed the co-worker who takes an hour to decide what to eat for lunch or what to purchase online? Then he/she complains about having to work late. This all goes back to prioritizing.

* *Time is precious.*
  Try and spend it as best as possible.

It's the one thing in life that we cannot get back once is has passed. Make the most of your time. Work during 'work time', relax during 'downtime', have fun during 'fun time'. You get the picture. Too many of us let each day go by, without actually putting any thought into it.

*Ask yourself, "what do I want to do today?" Do this each day.
Get the most out of each day.*

Working productively will allow for more personal time. Isn't that what we ideally want? Strive towards achieving it. 🍓

Chapter 7

Don't Become a Dinosaur

TAKE CHANCES

KEEP CHANGING

KEEP GROWING

I can't stress the importance of taking chances in your career and in your life, but let's just stick to the career stuff.

You need to keep reinventing yourself.

You need to keep yourself motivated.

It's not an easy thing to do. Think about it - how many of you dread going to work in the morning. You don't want to see your supervisor, manager and/or co-workers. You feel trapped. Worse, you feel bored. We all feel like that. I think this is probably even more common in a setting where you don't focus on creativity. The field of finance, for example, doesn't leave much room for imagination. So, what do most of us do? We go home, we complain about our day, about being unappreciated, or overworked.

What separates followers from leaders? Taking chances! Leaders are not afraid to take a chance. No one likes to make the wrong decision. No one likes to fail. Leaders would rather face these consequences than never take a chance at all. I don't mean be foolish about it. Obviously, there are some things that you shouldn't be impulsive about. However, there comes a time when you need to 'pull the trigger' on certain decisions or urges. Ask for that promotion. The biggest piece of advice that I have always given is to never stop interviewing, even if you're happy with your job. This just keeps you on your toes, and does not make you fearful of change.

Change can be synonymous with self-improvement, if you have a positive outlook on it.

Things don't always happen the way we plan them to happen. Curve balls get thrown at us along the way. The people who move on are the ones that can handle the curve balls, reflect, learn from these experiences, and move-on. You have to keep growing. If you don't keep growing, you will get stagnant in your career. This is what we call the 'dinosaurs' at work. They just continue to believe that their way is the best and only way. I've always admired those people whom I've worked with that always looked for a better way to meet their goals.

Keep yourself up-to-date with changes in your industry.

I'm a huge Madonna fan (I loved the eighties), not only because of her music, but because of her longevity in one of the toughest industries, the music industry. Madonna is a master of reinventing herself. The same stands for any industry if you want to get ahead at work, stay on-top, not get stale, and keep up with changes. Try to reinvent yourself at work, regardless of what it is you do, to keep you fresh. This will stop you from becoming a 'work dinosaur'.

Take continuing education courses to keep up with such changes.

Take courses or training sessions to keep up with technology changes.

Take chances!

Changing and growing are both essential. You can't have one without the other. It's a domino effect, the effect being at its greatest when you focus on your self improvement.

When I got 'laid-off' by my prior employer, I felt like I got hit on the head with a baseball bat.

Boy, talk about a blow to the ego.

It was one of my most humbling experiences. It was the perfect time for me to just allow myself to breakdown.

I had a choice.

I could have a meltdown (people would understand) or I could take a chance and try to grow as a professional. Believe me, I gave both a lot of thought. It's a lot easier to 'throw in the towel' and allow life to get the best of you at times. It was definitely harder to come to terms with change and to take a chance and start my own company. It wasn't easy.

We get stagnant when we stop focusing on professional growth. I don't necessarily mean growth in profits (although that would be nice too), but instead growth as an individual. This all rolls into your career as well. You need to stop and take the time to re-address and re-prioritize your goals. If you don't do this, the days start rolling up into the months and the months start blending into the years.

You need to make goals that will somewhat 'force the issue' on changing. Set new goals. Try something different. Learn another area in your field. Don't become stagnant. That's where continuing education comes in. Offer to assist another department or take on an additional project. Go to seminars and conferences. All of this helps you make sure that you do not become 'a dinosaur' yourself one of these days.

My business partner and I have to periodically stop and make the time to sit down and talk to each other about the direction of the company. We need to make time to do this, otherwise months go by without us truly communicating with one another. It's ironic how two people can see each other all the time, but not truly talk to or communicate with one another. I know it happens in a lot of relationships. Well, it happens at work as well. Don't wait for your annual evaluation to set goals with your manager.

Be proactive.

Present your peers with new ideas.

Revamp your workday.

The worst thing is when each workday seems exactly like the one from the day before, and will probably be the same as the one on the next day. It's really hard to stay motivated when you feel like this. Even as the company owner, when I feel myself 'getting stale', I still try and create new reports or marketing material in order to keep my mind sharp and be somewhat creative.

I hate being bored.

Taking chances and making changes are definitely two of the best ways that I have found to fight boredom, while being smart about it.

Challenge yourself.

Don't be afraid.

How NOT to become a dinosaur at work:

※ Try to reinvent yourself from time to time. It helps keep you motivated and 'fresh'. It helps you from becoming stagnant in your career. There's nothing worse than each workday being as bland as the last.

※ *Don't be afraid of making a decision.* Very often, no decision is the wrong one.

※ Leaders take chances!

※ Change can be synonymous with self improvement.

✳ *A positive outlook is everything!* Try and view a change as a positive event, even if it does not seem like one initially. You never know what will follow.

✳ Stay on top of changes in your field – go on an interview, speak to a headhunter from time to time, take continuing education classes.

✳ Set goals in priority. Review your goals periodically. Re-prioritize them if your objectives have changed.

✳ Try and stay creative. Take a different approach sometimes. Create a 'new' way to complete a task. Fight the same 'ho-hum' at work.

✳ Take the time to reflect, change and grow! ♟

Chapter 8

Don't Be Too Modest!

GO AHEAD AND FLAUNT YOUR STUFF!

I have made one definite observation throughout my career. Now let me remind you, the majority of my peers have been male. As a Sales Manager I managed both men and women and as an employer I have hired both sexes. One thing is for certain, men are better at 'flaunting it' than women are. We can learn a thing or two from them on this topic.

In my experiences as a woman, working with women, managing women and exchanging 'work stories' with my female friends in all professions, I have come to recognize a commonality amongst us – *women tend to be way too modest in the workplace!*

Ladies, learn from the men around you!

We don't give them enough credit in this arena. Men very often tend to over-inflate their tasks and achievements. I'm giving them kudos for doing this.

Most women I have encountered in business tend to do just the opposite. We work really hard, do really well, put in all of our effort, and then expect to be recognized and rewarded as a result of our labor. The problem is - this is often not the case. It's the 'work hard now, hopefully I'll get compensated later' philosophy. We need to work on this.

Women tend to be too modest.

Ladies, there is nothing wrong with being direct and assertive, especially when you are good at what you do. *GO AHEAD AND FLAUNT IT!* There is nothing wrong with being proud of, acknowledging, and, even vocalizing our achievements. Go ahead and brag sometimes! But, there's a time and place for everything. Bragging to co-workers gets you nowhere, and, just isn't a nice thing to do. But, shooting an email to your supervisor or manager about your accomplished tasks, that gets you leverage for your next review.

When you receive a compliment for your work, the best, and most underused answer is a simple 'thank you'. Learn to take credit gracefully, yet firmly. I'm sure you've all encountered a number of women that counter a compliment with an excuse. It can be as simple as complimenting someone that for looking like they lost weight and hearing them shoot off their meal plan or exercise regiment in defense. Take it in stride, be proud, and, just say 'thank you'. No need to 'lay it on too thick'. Just be confident instead.

No need to lie about what you've created at work, or improved, or questioned, or suggested or implemented. Instead, take credit for it. Do not wait for credit to be given. If you do receive credit, be proud and acknowledge yourself! If someone else receives the credit, document it.

More often than not, men tell you what they think they are worth, ask to be rewarded first and perform later. Women, on the other hand, wait to be rewarded. We work really hard, and expect it to be recognized, acknowledged and then rewarded. Well ladies, it doesn't always work that way. I'm sure many of you are nodding your heads as your reading this.

As a manager, when I conducted reviews for my male subordinates, they came into that meeting like squeaky wheels. They had no hang-ups about telling me everything that they 'sacrificed for the job'. They never held back about how hard they felt that they worked and were very direct about the compensation they expected to receive. The key word here is 'direct'. Women, on the other hand, were either on one end of the spectrum of being just way too aggressive and 'in your face' (to put it mildly), or, were willing to work really hard 'in silence' to move ahead, hoping to be compensated for it eventually. The difference here is 'firmly asking' versus 'hoping/expecting'.

Let me break this out into some bullet points and try to be as clear as I can.

❋ The squeaky wheel does often get the oil at work. If you feel that you have accomplished a well-done task, toot your horn about it! Don't just tell your co-workers. Tell your manager/

supervisor and tell their manager about it. Put it in writing. In other words, leave a paper trail of your accomplishments. Make them known! Don't wait for your manager to realize it. Be proactive. Your manager may be working on so many other projects and is not intentionally ignoring your success. Make it known to him/her. A good manager will appreciate this. But, make sure you can back-up your claims. In other words, do a good job and tell your higher-ups about it in writing.

✳ Make it known to your manager and/ or specific department heads where it is you want to go in the company. Make sure it's in writing. Be precise as to what your goals and objectives are within your career. Make them known. If you're happy in your position, reiterate that as well. In other words, be clear with your manager if you're happy with your job. But, if you want to move within the company, make it known where it is you want to be. (Don't forget the 'put it in writing' part of it)

※ Be prepared for your review. Make sure you assess your own accomplishments, and ideas, if you have any. Most importantly, ask for what you want. For example, if you want more money, ask for it. Tell your employer what it is you think you are worth. Be honest with yourself first before doing this. Do your homework. Be well aware and informed about your industry, whatever that industry may be. Most importantly, be clear with your objectives and requests.

✳ If you are given more responsibility, get compensated for it. Don't hope for it. Ask for it immediately. If you hear 'no' the first time, keep asking for it periodically. The squeaky wheel will get the oil first. Do not be passive if you can back up your request for more compensation. Do not be embarrassed to ask for more money. It simply reiterates that you take your responsibilities and your job seriously and are treating it like business.

✳ Never stop treating it like business. I'm not saying to be a robot; you need to find a balance between business, emotion, work, life, etc... But, work is business. Emotion can sometimes cloud that and make us forget the business aspect of work. Always be professional, whatever it is your requests or comments are.

I have studied my male co-workers very closely in this arena. They have no problem whatsoever flaunting their accomplishments, taking too much credit for them, or accepting congratulations. I commend them for that trait. If you work hard and/or are good at what you do, go ahead and flaunt it! But, do so at the right time, to the right people and keep it real. The only way to keep it real is by believing in yourself and in what you've accomplished. Do not downplay yourself at work. Take pride in your achievements. You've earned them and worked for them.

Don't be modest ladies! Be aware of 'what needs work', and work on it. Just the same, document, be vocal and be proud of what it is that 'you're good at'. 🐚

Chapter 9

Decide Your Self Worth

As you progress in your career, deciding your self worth grows in importance.

Being honest with yourself about the quality of your work is the first step. Applying this honesty will improve that quality and ensure your confidence. We often feel that we're not appreciated, that we're carrying all of the workload, that we can do a better job than our supervisor, that we should be making more money, etc...

You have to believe in yourself! I know we've all heard this before. It is so hard to do at times. But, if you don't believe in yourself, how do you expect your employer, supervisors, or clients to believe in your ability? It takes a lot of self focus and self reassurance.

Be your biggest critic, but know when to reward yourself as well. Don't beat yourself up over a mistake, or over a bad day, or a bad meeting. It happened, learn from it, and move on. We tend to dwell on everything. We're so busy dwelling that even a small bump in the road becomes a big mountain. Stop dwelling and move on.

The worst thing is to stop moving. Keep focused towards your goals and objectives, both short-term and long-term.

In deciding your self worth by being completely honest with yourself, you become equipped to confidently ask for that raise, that bigger bonus, or that promotion. Even if you do not get what you ask for, you have planted the seed. Ask for it again. When it gets to the point that you truly feel that your job is not measuring up to your expectations and standards, start putting your resume together.

I mentioned in a previous chapter the importance of interviewing from time to time throughout your career. This prevents you from getting rusty at interviewing. Most importantly, it reminds you that there may be something else out there, in case you do truly become dissatisfied at your current company.

A girlfriend of mine called me recently. She was very upset by the compensation package that she was offered within her organization. She was transitioning from salary to commission, and she was being completely low-balled in what she was offered. My advice to her was to remove her emotions from the equation and to counterattack with her mind instead.

I have given this advice to a number of my friends out of my own experience.

I'll give you an example: About eight years into my career, I felt it was time to take more control of my compensation. I had learned a lot from working around very hard-core, no-frills men. You can learn from them, you know. When I interviewed with the last company I was with, before I started my own company, I had decided that on my interview, I would ask them for a specific minimum salary that I expected.

I didn't budge.

They tried to offer me less.

I still didn't budge.

I knew that I had given them a figure that I felt I deserved and that I would be able to make them realize that I was worth that amount, if given the chance to prove myself. I have to tell you, on the inside, I wanted to crawl into a shell and hide under my covers. On the outside, I portrayed confidence in my abilities and in the experience that I would be bringing to the organization.

Guess what? It worked!

After that, I realized that these guys whom I worked around, these guys who always pressed for more money and higher bonuses, may have been on the right track.

It's business. Their offer had nothing to do with her personality. Very often in business, your employer or manager simply 'puts in out there' to see if you would bite. If you do, it's more money in their pockets. If you do not, then they expect you to counter-offer. Aim high! What's the worse that they could say? No? So what! It sets the negotiating game at a higher limit.

Don't expect your manager or employer to decide what you are worth. Your work should be a reflection of what you are asking for.

Aim high!

But, be honest with yourself.

One of my close friends, who happens to be one of the best managers I know, constantly negotiates compensation deals with potential employees based on setting benchmarks and targets. He tells the interviewee point blank that he/she can make the money that they are seeking to make, and more so, based on their productivity and output. However, he starts them out at a lower level. He gives them a high ceiling to work towards, but puts the ball in their court to do so. He wants to employ those individuals that are confident enough in themselves to realize that they will make more money in the long run, through their work and contribution to the company.

So, next time you are interviewing, or have your annual review, let your manager know how much you really want to get paid or where exactly you see yourself within the company. Many times, unless you ask for it, or are clear about your expectations, you may never achieve what you're seeking. ♡

Chapter 10

Don't Dwell On the Past

I love the fabulous quote, 'the past is history, the future a mystery, the current is a gift, that's why they call it the present.'

There's a big difference between dwelling on the past and learning from the past. Dwelling on the past makes you dormant to the present and future.

It keeps you in the past.

Learning from it requires a greater honesty, in which you ask yourself, 'What made me do that?' or 'Why was I more assertive then?', 'How did I get through that?', 'What would I do differently if I did it again?' and so on. This can obviously be applied to your business and personal decisions. At work, we often complete a project and get critiqued by everyone but ourselves. Look at the final output objectively. It's best to do this after a few weeks of completing a project or presentation, so that you can remove yourself emotionally from your evaluation and look at it logically. What would you say about your work if someone else had completed it instead of you?

Then, of course, there are bigger decisions that we look at: Career changes, our choice of employer, employee interactions, and of course, one's everyday wellbeing. Don't underestimate that last one. If there is something about a career decision you made in the past that you now wish you could change, then concentrate on changing it in the present.

Do not just 'throw in the towel' and stay where you are in your career because of a past decision. Do not stay at your job if you're no longer happy being there today, simply because you chose to work there five years ago. Do not keep a career that you're not happy with because you of a major you choose in college over a decade ago.

Look at the pros and cons of making changes to your past decisions. I get so saddened when I hear someone in their thirties refer to their twenties as the best time of their lives. Try and make each year the best one that you can. If you think you were already at the 'best' of your life, you're dwelling. That makes you stagnant! Stagnant makes you boring! Life is too short to be bored!

Of course, we're going to make some wrong decisions, as we will right ones. For some reason, we tend to dwell on the wrong ones much more than on the right ones. Why is this? If you fall into this category, try and be fair to yourself by at least dwelling on both the right and wrong decisions. But instead of dwelling, learn from both. There are times in my life when I have gotten myself through some pretty 'rough spots'. When I stop and look back, I can't believe that it was actually me, going through them and getting through them. I have to stop and analyze myself and learn from my own strength and will.

Our own strength and will often get lost in everyday life. I'm sure there are times at work when we go into 'robot' mode and do what needs to be done in order to move forward, because of what we may be going through in our personal lives, be it a marriage, a divorce, a death, or so on. During 'robot mode' there is no time to really think about everything that is going on in your life; you're just trying to make it through the day at work without having a breakdown. But, when the time is right, make sure you reflect on your feelings and grow from getting to know yet another side of yourself. ❈

Chapter 11

Make Peace With Yourself

After being in investment sales and management for over 15 years, all I can say is this – never sacrifice your morals or ethics for any position, promotion, recognition, bonus...you get the picture.

YOUR SELF-RESPECT IS ALL YOU ARE LEFT WITH AT THE END OF THE DAY. Positions get eliminated, companies get acquired, promotions get taken away, managers change, but all that can remain constant through this is one's self esteem, self worth, morals, and principles.

Do not shortchange yourself for your co-worker, or your manager.

Do not shortchange yourself to get a promotion. Next month, that position may be eliminated, and all you will be left standing with is your self-esteem.

Realize that there will be bumps along the road. There will be failures. Be open to them so that you can learn from them.

Be your hardest critic, but know when to reward yourself as well. You must be able to be honest with yourself in order to critique your work. Do not blame everyone around you for your own mistakes. There are no failures if you learn something and grow as a person and/or as a professional. Such circumstances become experiences, not failures.

Make peace with yourself about what type of employee, employer, manager, or co-worker that you are. Do you like who you are at work? This is very different from the question, "Do you like what you do at work?" 'Who you are' means: are you getting out of your career life the experiences that you seek to get? 'Who you are' doesn't ask 'what are you getting out of your career?' It asks, 'what do you want to get out of your career?' Are you in your career more so for the money, self-gratification, mental stimulation, power, or as a stepping stone? It may be a combination of a number of reasons. You need to know and understand why it is that you do what you do for over 40 hours a week.

Most importantly of all, DON'T FORGET TO LAUGH! Each year, as I get older, I realize that more and more people forget to laugh. Babies begin to smile and laugh at such at early age. They just wake up one morning and shock their parents by cracking their first smile. I'm sure that everyone can agree, that watching a baby laugh and smile is one of the most precious events.

Then things change. We grow up!

Through my own experiences, whether they were caused by sorrow, anger, business, or personal issues, I know that laughter has been the one consistent source of release that has helped me get through even the toughest moments. I believe in the saying, "if I don't laugh about it, I'm going to cry about it". I try and choose laughing over crying as often as I can. It helps sometimes to remove myself from my situation and view my life as if I were watching a television sitcom. Other times, it may be just stopping myself and laughing at how complex life can sometimes be. It was so much simpler when we were kids! Maybe it means laughing with someone else, at someone else, or just laughing at myself.

Laughter is crucial!

We forget how healthy it is to laugh. Laughter relieves stress. Laughter makes us feel alive again. Cracking a smile at a stranger can sometimes make us forget about the crowded rush hour commute. I know this all sounds 'hokey', but think about it. I'm sure all of you can name a handful of people with whom you work with on a daily basis whom you have never heard laugh or have never seen smile. Do you want to be one of those people?

Laughing makes me feel young and innocent again. Go to the park one day, and sit on a bench. Watch a group of children playing. Listen to the laughter that fills that air. It's soothing. It makes us yearn for the days when we can run around in the playground and laughed with our friends.

Laughter does not have to stop as we get older. I think as I get older, I have more things to laugh at about myself than I ever did. I really think laughing at myself is key. Everyone should be one of his or her best sources of entertainment. Instead of being aggravated over something 'stupid', look at the humor at it. I think that as we have more life experiences, we have more chances to laugh at 'bloopers' that come along the way.

Laughing is also contagious. So is not laughing. Have you ever noticed that you usually see a group of women at a bar or restaurant that are either all laughing, or not laughing at all? What group do you want to be in?

I know you've heard this all before. But take a moment to think about what I am saying. Have life's challenges made you so bitter that you don't even laugh or smile anymore? If so, take the time to work on this. Be conscious of this and put an effort into trying to smile or laugh at least once a day. Smiling and laughing are the best things out there for your health and mental well-being. On a personal note, it will just make you feel better, and makes those around you feel better as well. On a professional note, it makes you sometimes recognize your own mistakes, or deal with your co-workers, clients, or supervisors with more ease. It also helps keep you in a better mood and better spirits, which always leads to being more productive.

I find that laughing has not only gotten me through some of my biggest challenges professionally, but personally as well. Instead of blowing up over certain situations, I take a deep breath, and look at the flip side of things. You know those days you say to yourself, 'I can't believe the day I'm having' or 'this can only happen to me' – these are the best times to look at yourself and challenge your sense of humor. Make a funny story out of moments like these.

Let me give you an example (and hopefully make you laugh at the same time): I fly a lot for work. When we first started our company, I was flying up to 3 times a week all over the United States. I was scheduled to go see a prospect that was located about 4 ½ hours away by car. I wanted to make it a day trip, so I decided to fly instead of drive. I booked my airline ticket, and needed to be at the airport by 6am! I took a car service to the airport (about

30 minutes away), went through Security with my boarding pass, and approached the agent behind the desk regarding my seat assignment. I asked if I could be seated in bulk head. The agent informed me that there was no bulk head available on this trip. I inquired. Her answer was, "there is no bulk head available because you're actually booked to take a bus". You can imagine my confusion! "An airbus?", I asked. "No, a bus". "Does this bus have wings?" was my next question. The agent, with a dead straight serious face, just answered, "no". "Then what am I doing at an airport, with an airport boarding pass, at an airline gate?" was my response. I was livid for the first few seconds, after realizing that I wasted my time getting to the airport, my money booking a flight, and worst of all, this agent was looking at me like I was crazy! I took a deep breath,

took a step back and started laughing my head off. It was hilarious! I thought I was on candid camera! I used logic instead of emotion, saved the anger, rented a car, called my prospect, had a good laugh with him, decided to just drive, and just made the best of it.

At the end of it all, we're all mortals. We all want to feel that we served some type of purpose and that we made something of our lives. We all want peace for ourselves. Your career is just a piece of the puzzle...make it a worthwhile piece for yourself.

Chapter 12

Never End a Business Book in Chapter 11!